TO: FROM:

WHAT

EXTRAORDINARY

PEOPLE

KNOW

HOW TO CUT THE BUSY B.S.
AND LIVE YOUR *KICK-ASS* LIFE

ANTHONY MOORE

Internal images © pages 3, 7, 15, 23, 37, 55, 65, 71, 79, 89, 97, 105, 117, 127,
135, 136, R.Tsubin/Getty Images; page 14, JGI/Jamie Grill/Getty Images;
page 41, yulkapopkova/Getty Images

Internal images on pages vi, 6, 10, 16, 20, 22, 26, 29, 32, 34, 36, 44, 48, 51,
54, 58, 63, 64, 70, 73, 75, 76, 78,86,88, 96, 103, 111, 115, 116, 119, 122, 124,
131, and 134 have been provided by Pexels and Pixabay; these images are
licensed under CC0 Creative Commons and have been released by the
author for public use.

Published by Simple Truths, an imprint of Sourcebooks
P.O. Box 4410, Naperville, Illinois 60567-4410
(630) 961-3900
sourcebooks.com

Printed and bound in China.
OGP 10 9 8 7 6 5 4 3 2 1

TO KiMi,

for believing in me when I didn't
believe in myself.

TABLE OF

CONTENTS

PART 1.

You Are Currently Stuck

FOR MOST OF MY life, I lived in a cage of mediocrity.

That's the best way I can describe it. It was a prison cell, and all my fears of looking stupid, worries about the future, and anxiety about being "chosen"—by cute girls, my boss, my family, sports coaches, the cool kids—kept me living as the barest, slimmest act of my true self. I walked through the halls of my high school as a fifteen-year-old student, but inside, I was a terrified little boy, watching life unfold from the safety of my mind.

I eventually escaped this prison, but this jailbreak took many years. Now, I see other captives masquerading as free men and women, people who don't even know they're living life behind bars.

You are currently stuck. And if you want to get out, you need to understand how this cage works—and how the hell you ended up in it.

WHAT IS THE MEDIOCRITY TRAP?

> "Those who will not govern themselves are condemned to find masters to govern over them."
>
> —STEVEN PRESSFIELD

THE MAJORITY OF PEOPLE are living lives that are below their potential. The result? Most of us are unfulfilled.

How can I say that?

Well, to start with, most of us don't have great relationships. Despite living in an age where you can connect to almost anyone at any time, most Americans claim to have an average of only two close friends. In addition, despite the technology that allows for more dating opportunities and connections, it is harder than ever to find "the one." Even if you do, half of marriages end in divorce. Do you think the other 50 percent are living the life of their dreams? No! Of that 50 percent, maybe a tenth can say they have an incredible, amazing, fulfilling marriage.

What's more, while the old saying used to be "at least I have my health," most of us don't! Most people's health is average at best. In the United States, many are ailing or in decline. In spite of record numbers of gyms, juice bars, and diet programs, we are as unhealthy as ever. Twenty-nine million Americans have diabetes, one in five children are clinically obese, and only about 16 percent of women and 32 percent of men don't worry about their weight. A mere one in seven people report waking up feeling refreshed after sleeping.

Our careers aren't much better. Most of us don't like

or particularly care about our jobs, despite them being where we spend most of our waking hours! Gallup's oft-cited 2017 State of the American Workplace study reveals that over 87 percent of people aren't engaged at work. Yikes.

For the most part, we live bearable lives. They're "good enough." There are few highs or lows; life resembles a relatively steady line, one neither particularly great nor awful.

But do you know what a flat line on an EKG means?

It means you're dead.

This complacency we all settle for is something I have termed the "Mediocrity Trap." And it's time to get the hell out.

The reason most people live, in author David Deida's words, a "relatively secure and comfortable, but dead" life is simple: it's easy, safe, and familiar. But it's still a dead life.

WHY EVERYONE REMAINS STUCK

"Is there a difference between average and mediocre? Not so much."

—SETH GODIN

EVERY DAY, MILLIONS OF people wake up to a dull life characterized by shallow relationships, mundane jobs, low incomes, muffin tops, uncontrollable insecurity, and endless worry about when it's all going to stop. They change slowly and unconsciously over time—and not for the better.

They know something is wrong. There's a constant whisper in the back of their minds that reminds them of this, a voice that can't be silenced.

Very few people act to silence that never-ending stream of anxiety. But there's good news: if you bought this book and are reading this, *you* are taking the first step toward change! You're part of the minority that's actually seeking improvement. But the majority of people won't. Why? If they know something is wrong, why don't they change? Why don't they *do* something about it?

This happens for many reasons. Some people are just too scared. They don't want to rock the boat. "Better the devil you know than the devil you don't," they sigh as they tolerate another slap in the face from their mediocre, substandard environment. But this fear is powerful, and it can grow so powerful that it will dictate every decision you make. Robert Kiyosaki, bestselling author of *Rich Dad Poor Dad*, once wrote, "For many people, the power of their excuse is more powerful than their dreams." The fear of pain, the fear of failure, even the fear of succeeding can all become strong enough to dominate you into submission, into living a life founded on avoiding pain rather than seeking growth. Your ability to tolerate pain directly determines how successful you'll be. If you let it, fear of pain will freeze you as the current mediocre version of yourself, permanently. Thus, people remain in perpetual mediocrity.

Others are too distracted. They're so caught up in the mundane, trivial rhythms of email, traffic, work, the news, grocery shopping, cleaning the house, TV, and whatever their smartphone is buzzing about that they can't even see their lives have become unfulfilling and profoundly empty. From the moment they wake up to the moment they fall asleep, their eyes are drawn to the short term. In short, they're "busy." But as essayist Tim Kreider once wrote, "Busyness serves as a kind of existential reassurance, a hedge against emptiness; obviously your life cannot possibly be silly or trivial or

meaningless if you are so busy, completely booked, in demand every hour of the day."

Busyness is often a sign of weakness, a cluttered mind unable to set boundaries. When you're too busy, it means you haven't set up boundaries to focus on the important things. This constant concentration on trivial, unimportant matters leads to emptiness and sadness. The ancient Stoic philosopher Seneca once warned, "Love of bustle is not industry." The love of busyness only leads you quicker to the grave.

Some people remain in mediocrity because they're just too prideful: they like being the big fish in their small pond (even if their pond is dirty and full of toxic waste). They know they need to change, but they don't want to start over and learn the new skills required to succeed on higher levels. Even though their life is totally miserable, they reassure themselves with phrases like "At least *I'm* in charge." They're fine with mediocrity as long as they're the ones calling the shots. But this is like a little toddler wearing a soiled diaper thinking, "I know it smells awful, but it's soft and it's mine." So people choose to be the captain of a canoe with holes in the bottom instead of a student on a mighty yacht, sailing toward mastery and greatness.

But by far the most common reason most people never rearrange their cruddy life: they simply can't be bothered.

Most people are just too lazy to live happier lives. Let that sink in for a second: the main reason most people end up unsuccessful is because they couldn't be bothered to do the work. They are *unwilling* to do the work. They know what they want; they might even know how to get there. They want to have 100 percent financial freedom, be their own boss, own a company, travel the world, lose weight, open a business, write a book, and a hundred other dreams. But dreams take work over a long time, and the process can be tedious. So most people remain in mediocrity because they are just too lazy.

Ironically, these individuals always seem to have enough energy to defend their low standards.

Whatever the reason, most people will remain in mediocrity. They won't avoid it. Years will go by, and most people will look back and wish they had started earlier. Feeling like it's too late to achieve your dreams is terrible but has become all but commonplace.

Feeling panicked? Depressed? Like a failure? Don't worry. I'm just giving you the bad news first. Trust me—once you know how the game works, you'll be ahead of 95 percent of the competition. But before you can excel in any area, you need to know what you're up against. I haven't even gotten to the worst part: the world actually *sets you up* for mediocrity.

I'm happy to report that you can break the cycle. I have done so myself, as have thousands of others. However, in order to do so, there is still one more thing you need to understand…and that's that the game is set up against you. The world, society as a whole, actually *wants* you to stay in the trap.

THE WORLD AND MEDIOCRITY

"Take into account that you have been educated with restrictions. Be aware of this so that you don't underestimate the possibilities."

—GRANT CARDONE

THE WORLD DOES NOT want you to succeed.

No, the world has one agenda when it comes to you: The world wants you to *pay*.

How? Frankly, there's a fortune to be made off

your distraction and trying to fit in with everyone else. Television, streaming services, movie studios, social media, apps, video games, smartphone companies, and countless other billion-dollar industries have but one goal:

To make money from your attention.

This doesn't even include all the other industries that are set up to rope you into keeping up with the

Joneses. Real estate companies want you to buy (doesn't matter if you can't afford it). Banks want you to open more credit cards (even if you're already in severe debt). Tech companies want you to purchase the latest gadget (even if you just bought the last version). App and media companies want to keep you watching, playing, scrolling, clicking (even if you only have so much free time and they already own half of it). Outdated structures like the broken education and loan system, the fixed-in-office nine-to-five workday schedule, and endless amounts of addictive entertainment set you up to pay exorbitant amounts of time and money on things to keep you occupied while you unknowingly slide into the Mediocrity Trap.

The world isn't concerned with making you successful. Frankly, the world couldn't care less if you achieve your dreams. In fact, in many cases, achieving your dreams would be detrimental to the system as it stands—one less cog to count on.

All of this is not intended to be bleak; I'm here to show you how to cheat the system. Rather than kick your legs out from under you, what I want you to understand is this: if you follow all the rules, buy what everyone else buys, act the way everyone else acts, and live the life everyone else is living, you're almost guaranteed to end up in mediocrity.

But as we now know and the data continue to prove time and time again, most of the world isn't happy! We live in a world where most people have not accomplished what they really want to do. Hell, most people aren't even on track. They aren't living their ideal lives. Far from it. Most people are living small little lives defined by consumption and distraction that are, frankly, mediocre.

The solution? Do what people are unwilling to do. If you want what you've never had—be it financial, emotional, spiritual, mental, physical—then the answer is simple: you have got to do what you have never done before. Fortunately, this process isn't complicated at all.

PART 2.

Breaking Free of the Trap

NOT EVERYONE HAS AMBITIOUS dreams to be extraordinary. Not everyone is as obsessed as you or me with becoming our best selves and going to sleep every night knowing we were as courageous, creative, loving, and truly *ourselves* as possible.

If you're ready to start living that life, good. It's about time. Here's how to break out and upgrade your life into an extraordinary one—for good.

CHANGE YOUR ENVIRONMENT
OR IT'LL CHANGE YOU

"If we do not create and control our environment,
our environment creates and controls us."

—MARSHALL GOLDSMITH

MOST OF US HAVE a similar approach to change. Something happens that gets us pumped up and motivated— maybe it's watching your friend graduate medical school, maybe it's watching *Gladiator*—and this surge of adrenaline and motivation spurs us to make a powerful vow: "Screw it, I'm losing forty pounds." "Time to quit this dead-end job." For the next little while, the vow apparently works; we start eating healthy, going to the gym, applying for new jobs.

But after a few weeks, our motivation wanes. That adrenaline of starting something new is gone. It's not novel anymore; it's just *hard*. After a few weeks of half-assing it, most of us slip back into the same mediocre behaviors that we were stuck in before.

This has happened to me countless times. I've started going to the gym at least a dozen times since college. I've bought expensive moleskin journals to write in that go untouched after the first week. I'm sure many of you can relate.

All of us have a cycle of repeated failure, but we keep coming back for more. We want to change, but we just can't seem to break free of the cycle. And we each have our own triggers and traps that make up our cycle. For myself, the most prominent cycle of repeated failure I faced was through an addiction that

I allowed to ruin my life for years before getting things under control. Since massive exposure in my youth, I was a porn addict for nearly twenty years before finally breaking the cycle through a twelve-step program that stuck. While such an addiction may seem innocuous to some, I can assure you that, left unchecked, it can destroy nearly every aspect of your life. By breaking this addiction and living clean, I was first exposed to the idea of what real change can provide. This lesson and the promise of lasting change in other areas of my life—change that broke my failure cycle—shifted everything for me…and it can for you too.

Here's the simple lesson from this chapter: *If you want to change something, you need to change your environment first.*

The forty-year-old alcoholic who wants to quit can't keep any alcohol in the house. The overweight twenty-something who wants a six-pack can't keep junk food in the house. If you want change, you have to change your environment first.

We waste immense energy and willpower saying no to options we should remove entirely. Bestselling author David Kadavy once remarked, "When you build a habit, you don't have to spend mental energy deciding what to do." If you give yourself an out, you will take it. Eventually. It's like someone clinging to a dangling rope. It doesn't matter how strong their hands are; they'll let go eventually. It's not a matter of willpower; it's a matter of designing an environment that makes failure almost impossible.

⫽ Don't Focus on Goals. Set Systems Instead.

> "I had to quit telling myself that I had innate discipline and fabulous natural self-control. That is a lie. I have to put systems and programs in place that make me do smart things."
>
> —DAVE RAMSEY

Goals suck.

They're hard. They take a ton of effort, a long time to get there, and even if you finally reach them, it's always a little hollow.

Setting goals is for beginners. Goals are for people who don't know how to design systems in an environment that makes success practically guaranteed. This is one of the most powerful secrets of the world's top performers.

James Clear, a powerfully motivating favorite author of mine, had this to say on systems versus goals:

I just added up the total word count for the articles I've written this year... In the last twelve months, I've written over 115,000 words. The typical book is about 50,000 to 60,000 words, so I have written enough to fill two books this year.

All of this is such a surprise because I never set a goal for my writing. I didn't measure my progress in relation to some benchmark. I never set a word count goal for any particular article. I never said, "I want to write two books this year."

What I did focus on was writing one article every Monday and Thursday. And after sticking to that schedule for eleven months, the result was 115,000 words. I focused on my system and the process of doing the work. In the end, I enjoyed the same (or perhaps better) results.

What Clear is saying here is groundbreaking. All of us have had goals to write a book, lose twenty pounds, start our own company, pay off our student loans, whatever the case may be. But instead of setting a goal and inching our way toward it, always fighting off the despair of no evidential progress, we should instead design a *system* that produces consistent progress every day.

When I graduated college, I had $16,000 in student loans (statistically, a paltry sum, as that is far below the average). Low in comparison or not, I hated being in debt. I wanted to pay it off as quickly as possible. At first, I was busting my butt to put in $50 a week. (I distinctly remember walking down the street to the bank every payday and sadly depositing my pitiful few bucks in the ATM.) I wasn't buying coffee or eating out, and I was subsisting solely on iced tea and chicken breasts at home to save money. I had a weekly goal, but it was awful to think of how long the larger goal would take. After six months of grueling discipline, I had paid off about 7 percent of it. At that rate, my interest rate would keep me in debt forever.

Over time, I gave up on the "set a goal this month" stuff altogether. It was too depressing. Instead, I worked to design a system that would enable my success. Basically, I laid out a plan to create a lifestyle that gave me maximum satisfaction along with maximum money toward the debt. I calculated exactly how much of my income I could live on (which included buying coffee—I hate not being able to buy coffee). It was about 70 percent, leaving me 30 percent to put toward my loans. Every month, I lived on 70 percent of my income (which got pretty easy after I got used to it—the benefit of living in a system). I started building momentum. It wasn't difficult—it was exhilarating. Every paycheck felt like punching my debt in the face. It was fun.

I eventually paid off my loans right before I turned twenty-five, and my wife and I refuse to ever get in debt again. It feels incredible and liberating. And I was able to achieve that not by goals but with a system.

The lesson here is simple: don't set goals; design systems instead. Design an environment that automatically enables small progress every day. Soon, you'll get to a point where you don't think about it. It takes no willpower at all. It's just your life.

Want to lose twenty pounds? Then start eating better and drinking water every day. Better yet, go for a jog. Don't think about it. Do it.

Want to write a book? Don't say, "I'm going to write a book by December 31." That's exhausting. (I'm already stressed just thinking about such a venture!) Just write every Monday and Thursday. Don't think about it. Do it.

Want to pay off your loans? Save up for a house? Win the championship for your adult soccer league? Create an Etsy store?

Don't set the goal. Design a system that gets you closer every day. Start going, start doing, and the results will follow faster than you could have believed possible. Setting a goal can create the feeling of impossibility for success. There can be daunting failures and drops in momentum. But by simply creating a new reality for yourself, you are setting yourself up for a new *self* entirely.

James Clear also said:

If you're a coach, your goal is to win a championship. Your system is what your

team does at practice each day.

If you're a writer, your goal is to write a book. Your system is the writing schedule that you follow each week.

If you're a runner, your goal is to run a marathon. Your system is your training schedule for the month.

If you're an entrepreneur, your goal is to build a million-dollar business. Your system is your sales and marketing process.

This is advanced thinking. Most people have goals but no idea how to design an environment that automatically attracts success.

If you want to be successful, design an environment that has systems that will make you succeed no matter what. Goals don't work; what works are systems in place that decrease the possibility of failure and increase the eventuality of success. What works is doing, not thinking about doing.

BE A REBEL
(A.K.A. EMBRACE THE WEIRD)

"It's no great achievement to go along with the crowd. Be the unusual guy, the extraordinary guy."

—DARREN HARDY

IF YOU WANT WHAT no one else has, you have to do what no one else does.

In short, be a rebel. Start doing weird things, things most people don't—or won't—do. It has often been said that "successful people do what unsuccessful people are unwilling to do."

Eat Weird Things

"Tell me what you eat, and I shall tell you what you are."

—JEAN ANTHELME BRILLAT-SAVARIN

What you eat frames your day. It's the structure that sustains your health, which is the foundation for your energy, focus, creativity, and endurance. What you eat enables you to create hyperfocused productivity...or disables you into a food coma.

Most people don't eat an optimal diet. Remember, the world sets you up for this. There's enormous money to be gained from your healthcare bill, prescription meds, exercise regimen, workout clothes, and fast-food budget. With a burger and fries being cheaper than an apple, the world doesn't set you up to eat well. In the words of Aubrey Marcus in his book *Own the Day, Own Your Life*: "If you are anything like I was...you found yourself owned by cravings and convenience, only to be left battling inflammation, brain fog, low energy, and mood dysregulation, all of which prevent you from crushing it during your afternoon work session." This is the norm.

In general, most people aren't health literate. They know they're not healthy but don't really know what to do instead. For the most part, people plan their diet based on outdated and archaic models like how many calories a meal contains or whether it's "natural" or "organic," famously ambiguous and purposely vague terms with no real meaning.

This section has a simple message: eat right. What that means is get your health under control and set up for your success (which probably means rebelling against what everyone else is eating). Everyone's body is different, and there is no perfect diet or nutrition plan. As Arnold Schwarzenegger, one of the most successful bodybuilders in history, once said, "You can't just copy someone else's routine, because everyone's body is different."

I'm not here to tell you what to eat—I'm not your doctor. Your body is different from mine. You don't need more *information* on how to improve your health. We are all aware of the basic premises for healthy living, and there is a wealth of information at your fingertips with options on how to go about healthy living against various ideals. As Derek Sivers once said, "If information was the answer, then we'd all be billionaires with perfect abs."

What you need is motivation to be more. The first step is changing your diet in whatever way works best for you. My suggestion is to make it sustainable over all else and to start small. Ain't no way you're giving up years of routine dieting this week.

What I want you to do is research a diet different from what most people around you eat. The phrase "if it's popular, it's wrong" comes to mind. Mark Twain put it another way: "Whenever you find yourself on the side of the majority, it is time to pause and reflect."

Are you eating what the average consumer is

eating? Are you using discipline with your diet or just eating what's in front of you? Are you happy with having the health everyone else has? If the answers to these questions are at odds with your own health, it's time to pause and reflect.

 Say Weird Things

"The bitterest tears shed over graves are for words left unsaid and deeds left undone."

—HARRIET BEECHER STOWE

When my wife and I were in premarital counseling, our counselor gave us a piece of advice that would end up changing our lives: Always make the first move.

The meaning is simple: if you can help the relationship (friendship, marriage, partnership, whatever), then do it. Don't wait for the other person to act (even if you want to).

Most people have strained and superficial relationships with friends, even with family. This is because most people always wait for the other person to make the first move, say hello, organize a hangout, or apologize. They are not willing to say what needs to be said to nurture the relationship.

This is a pride thing. It's one of the main killers of marriages, friendships, and even families.

If you want to have deep, meaningful relationships with your friends, family, and even just the people in your day-to-day life, make the first move—even if it should be them. Be the first to:

▶ Initiate the conversation

▶ Send the first text

▶ Say you miss them

▶ Say you love them

▶ Apologize and ask for forgiveness

▶ Organize a hangout

▶ Compliment them

▶ Thank them

▶ Tell them you appreciate what they did

For a long time, I felt awkward and uncomfortable telling my brothers and sister "I love you." Three of the people whom I loved most in the entire world, and I couldn't say it!

Now, I tell them I love them all the time. I say it over text, over casual phone calls, at crises and celebrations, and over the holidays. I tell my friends too. Every single important person in my life—mentors, family, friends, even coworkers—know how special they are to me.

It feels silly to be afraid to say this to a loved one. Yet so many people can't say a few simple words that would galvanize the entire relationship and deeply touch their soul.

Once you start doing the unusual yet critical work of simply saying it, you can begin enjoying a gem most people never will: close, loving, life-giving relationships with many people.

⫽ Spend Your Time in Weird Ways

"[Successful people] don't see it as 'free time,' actually. They see it as the only time they have to do the things they really want to do in life—and they don't take a minute for granted."

—NICOLAS COLE

I love TV shows. (If you can quote *Arrested Development* or *The Simpsons*, we're already best friends.) I love lounging on the couch. I love spending hours doing nothing. These are not inherently bad things. The problem is that most people aren't responsible enough to spend their time this way without becoming lazy, complacent, and tired. Without letting their time spent on these activities run amok.

You don't have much free time. If you're like most people and you spend it watching television, scrolling through social media, and generally trying to "check out" mentally in any way possible (recreational drugs, alcohol, sex/porn, etc.), you're going to stay stuck in mediocrity with most people. If you want to improve your life in some way, it starts with how you spend your free time.

This doesn't happen all at once—almost nothing starts that way. Everything is hard before it's easy, and you need to ease your way into something sustainable. Marketing gurus Neil Patel, Patrick Vlaskovits, and Jonas Koffler put it this way: "Getting ahead is based on manageable tweaks, not tectonic shifts."

The world's most successful people are extremely intentional with their free time. The top one percent of performers, earners, and leaders don't squander their free time—which for all of us is the only time we have to improve ourselves—in the silly ways the majority does. They see their free time as the only time they have to master themselves and learn new skills to help build their empires.

The fun part about starting to use your free time productively is when you actually *do* rest and relax. It's

indescribably more enjoyable to crack open a six-pack of beer in front of the TV with some friends when you know without a doubt you've been using your free time to become more successful.

When you're spending your time the way everyone else is—sleeping, bingeing on TV, complaining, zoning out—it's time to reflect. If you want what no one else has, you must do what no one else does. Choose to reinvest your free time into expanding your future, not spending it in ways you can never get back.

Spend Your Money in Weird Ways

"Live like no one else now, so later you can live like no one else."

—DAVE RAMSEY

After reading dozens of the top finance and personal development books, I realized all these books were saying the same things, just in different ways.

One of the most important finance lessons I learned was this: if you follow traditional financial wisdom, you'll probably never build wealth. Author Derek Sivers, founder of CD Baby ($100 million in sales), recounted this story:

Kimo Williams is this large, black man, a musician who attended Berklee School of Music and then stayed there to teach for a while... What he taught me got me to graduate in half the time it would [normally]

take. He said, "I think you can graduate Berklee School of Music in two years instead of four. The standard pace is for chumps. The school has to organize its curricula around the lowest common denominator, so that almost no one is left out. They have to slow down, so everybody can catch up. But," he said, "you're smarter than that." He said, "I think you could just buy the books for those, [skip the classes], and then contact the department head to take the final exam to get credit."

The lesson here is simple: the standard pace is for chumps. Most financial advice out there—save money, diversify your investments, pay off small credit charges every month—is designed to help the lowest common denominator, the average Joe with the least amount of financial sense.

Therefore, if you want to build wealth, be a rebel. Do weird things. Don't put all your eggs in one basket?

"Put all your eggs in one basket, and then watch the basket," said Andrew Carnegie, one of the richest men in the history of mankind. Diversify investments? Irving Kahn, a hugely successful investor who died at age 109, once quipped, "I would recommend that private investors tune out the prevailing views they hear on the radio, television, and the internet. They are not helpful." Warren Buffet agrees, saying, "A good investor has the opposite temperament to that prevailing in the market."

The standard pace is for chumps, and standard advice is meant for the lowest common denominator—this is not the stuff you follow if you want to become 100 percent financially independent.

Much like your health goals, there is an infinite supply of information on how you could get your money in order. Obviously, what works for you won't work for everyone. The key is simply finding something that *works*. To that end, I'll leave you with the seven most important finance books I've ever read:

The Millionaire Next Door: The Surprising Secrets of America's Wealthy by Thomas Stanley

2. *Think and Grow Rich* by Napoleon Hill

3. *The Science of Getting Rich* by Wallace Wattles

4. *The Richest Man in Babylon* by George Clason

5. *The Total Money Makeover: A Proven Plan for Financial Fitness* by Dave Ramsey

6. *I Will Teach You to Be Rich* by Ramit Sethi

7. *Rich Dad Poor Dad* by Robert Kiyosaki

6.

WHAT YOU BELIEVE ABOUT YOURSELF IS WHAT YOU BECOME

"Winners act like winners before they're winners."

—BILL WALSH

STRONG BELIEF ATTRACTS SUCCESS, but disbelief guarantees failure.

Richard Wiseman, a former street magician turned researcher and author, once conducted a simple study with two groups—one group of people thought of themselves as lucky, and the other self-proclaimed they were unlucky.

For the study, Wiseman placed a $20 bill on the street and had each member of each group walk past it. The group that believed they were lucky spotted the bill almost every time; the unlucky group almost always ignored it and walked right past!

In the words of British philosophical writer James Allen, "As [a man] thinks, so he is. As he continues to think, so he remains."

Success, in all its forms, isn't something you seize so much as it is something that is *attracted* to you. The easiest and most productive strategy for becoming a more successful person is to start believing you *already are*.

In his bestselling finance book *Rich Dad Poor Dad*, Robert Kiyosaki told a story of one of the first times he went totally broke. His business partner had left him with nothing, his investments were lost, and he was severely in debt. During this time, some subpar, mediocre business opportunities were presented to him. He still told his wife, "I am a rich man—and rich men don't do that!" Despite having literally zero money, he still carried himself as a rich man would.

Why? Because rich people act a certain way. They don't behave the way the mediocre, fearful masses do—they take risks. They improve their financial literacy. They say no to garbage opportunities, because that's what rich people do.

So how do you carry yourself?

Who do you believe you are?

To achieve success bigger than you've ever experienced, you first need the mental capacity for it. Until then, you'll probably never reach the level of success you've always wanted, and if you're unfortunate enough to inherit it without earning it first, you risk destroying your entire life. (How many "successful" people live horribly imbalanced and empty lives?)

Where to Start

"Belief, strong belief, triggers the mind to figure out ways and means and how-to."

—DR. DAVID SCHWARTZ

Once you start to believe, *really* believe, your brain starts operating under that assumption. Your brain operates under the rules of your belief system; if you want big success, your brain must believe it first. Everything your mind acts on is guided by your beliefs; if you don't believe, your brain takes that fact and acts accordingly.

The truth is, most people don't really believe they can achieve greatness. They don't believe they can actually live an extraordinary life. As a result, this becomes true; they aren't successful. They settle for good opportunities, believing great ones just don't come around. They don't *attract* opportunities. In fact, they actively miss them—even when they're right at their feet! As researcher Jim Collins wrote in his landmark book *Good to Great*:

Good is the enemy of great. And that is one of the key reasons why we have so little that becomes great. We don't have great schools, principally because we have good schools. We don't have great government, principally because we have good government. Few people attain great lives, in large part because it is just so easy to settle for a good life.

I love playing basketball. But in high school, I had a rude awakening. After playing for my whole life (thinking I was a pro), I found myself fighting for the last spot on the lowly freshman team with a guy I had assumed I could run circles around. I got the spot, but my confidence was shattered. Then I rode the bench all year.

For years, I subconsciously believed I couldn't

shoot the basketball well. This became obvious. During games, I would pass instead of taking a wide-open shot. I wouldn't even consider shooting. I was a bad shooter, I had told myself. My brain reacted accordingly.

Years later, I got sick of being such a passive, scared player. I began shooting again. Unsurprisingly, I shot a lot of air balls. But I got better. I had to tell myself, "I'm a good shooter. I'm a smart shooter. I make all my shots." I didn't make all of them, but they started going in! It was incredible. I couldn't believe it. I ditched my old, wrong beliefs and started believing something new.

If you believe—*truly* believe—something about yourself, it will become true. Your mind will figure out the means how.

Of course, belief by itself doesn't guarantee success. (Remember, I believed I was a great basketball player before I got to high school!) I believed an online writing course I created was a surefire five-figure launch success—until literally no one bought it.

I believed I was an incredible worker—until my boss fired me for not doing my job.

Belief is the first step. Action is next. Faith without works is dead; belief without action is pointless and ineffective. What you believe determines what your action will be.

If the most you ever think you'll make is minimum wage, you'll probably spend many years making only that (and perhaps a few bucks more from mandatory raises you never asked for). But if you think you're going to make $200,000 this year, your brain figures out how that's going to work.

Robert Kiyosaki has a simple exercise to develop your self-belief. Instead of saying the phrase, "I can't afford it," say this instead: "How can I afford it?" The first phrase ends the conversation; the second forces you to figure out how to succeed.

IF YOU WANT TO SUCCEED, YOU CAN'T JUST BE *INTERESTED*— YOU NEED TO BE *COMMITTED*

"If you're interested, you come up with stories, excuses, reasons, and circumstances about why you can't or why you won't. If you're committed, those go out the window. You just do whatever it takes."

—JOHN ASSARAF

EVERYONE WANTS TO CHANGE something about themselves, to improve something. They want a better job, more money, a better body, a calmer mind, better sleep.

But most people are merely interested in change; they're not actually committed to doing the required work.

Just because you're not 100 percent committed to something isn't bad. I like playing basketball, but I'm not 100 percent committed to going pro someday. I like the idea of having six-pack abs, but frankly, I'd rather enjoy drinking IPAs and eating immense amounts of Mexican food.

But if you want to change something, you need to sacrifice your apathy and upgrade from merely interested to actually committed.

People who are merely interested say things like this:

▶ I want to lose twenty pounds.

▶ I want to go to bed earlier.

▶ I should drink less coffee.

▶ I'm going to cut out dairy this month.

▶ I need a new job.

▶ I'm going to write a book this year.

None of these are specific, lasting, or measurable. They're not founded on a firm bedrock of motivation and commitment. This new change might've been made in a particularly pumped-up moment, but as Dr. Carol Dweck remarks in her book *Mindset: The New Psychology of Success*, "Vowing, even intense vowing, is often useless... What works is making a vivid, concrete plan."

People who are committed say things like this:

▶ I am someone who lives a healthy lifestyle.
▶ I am 100 percent committed to this twelve-week marathon training plan.
▶ I am canceling the next month's social engagements so I can focus solely on getting a new job.
▶ I will save $500 each month instead of spending it on bars and fast food.
▶ I will do whatever it takes.

Behavioral change and achieving success aren't complicated. Bestselling author and speaker Jim Rohn once said, "Success is neither magical nor mysterious. Success is the natural consequence of consistently applying basic fundamentals."

These fundamentals are enabled through commitment. Once you're committed to doing whatever it takes, you can work to achieve anything you want. Jim Rohn also said:

It's when a human with sufficient disgust, desire, and determination to change his life finally steps up to the bar of human justice and shouts for all the world to hear, "I have had it with defeat and humiliation, and I will tolerate it no longer." That is when time, fate, and circumstance call a hasty conference, and all three wearily agree, "We had best step aside, because we are powerless to stop that kind of resolve."

When you fully commit and act on that commitment, your environment comes to your aid. Obstacles suddenly disappear. Problems become opportunities, and bad luck upgrades to good favor.

Most people will never reach this level; they are not willing to do whatever it takes in nearly any area. You don't have to be a crazy zealot-guru to reach this level of intensity. You just have to commit. Then, don't break that commitment for anything.

Tim Grover, personal trainer to athletes like Michael Jordan and Kobe Bryant, once wrote, "People are always asking me about the secrets and tricks I use to get results. Sorry if this disappoints you: There are no secrets. There are no tricks... It's simple. Ask yourself where you are now, and where you want to be instead."

There are no tricks, life hacks, or one weird reason that will make you succeed. Either you're committed or just interested. If you want to succeed, you need to upgrade.

IF YOU TOLERATE MEDIOCRITY, THAT'S WHAT YOU GET

"Remember: we all get what we tolerate. So stop tolerating excuses within yourself, limiting beliefs of the past, or half-assed or fearful states."

—TONY ROBBINS

YOU GET WHAT YOU tolerate. If you tolerate mediocre circumstances that are merely good enough, that's what you'll get. But if you only tolerate excellence, if you only allow yourself to have high standards, that's what you'll achieve.

Dating is one of the most common examples of this. Back in college, I was lonely; I'd had girlfriends for years, but in my sophomore year, I found myself heartachingly single.

There was a girl I was involved with who had all kinds of warning signs: codependent, passive-aggressive, putting herself down while criticizing me. I later found out she had been sleeping with her ex while the two of us were dating.

But my standards were low enough that all that was fine by me. I tolerated her unbecoming, alarming behavior because it was more important for me to feel liked by a cute girl with glossy dark hair than to remain single. I got what I tolerated, and it ended in heartbreak and disaster.

What are you tolerating right now that you need to change? What areas of your life have very low standards? Are you willing to settle for an exceptionally crappy job, relationship, diet, or sleeping schedule because you're not willing to raise your standards?

What do you want? For me, I wanted an incredible romantic relationship, a successful writing career, better quality sleep (I've had sleep problems for years), and healing from my collection of personal and family issues that had left my emotions in a state of constant upheaval.

I had been tolerating mediocrity for a long time before I decided to raise my standards. No more dating losers—I would only tolerate extremely high-quality relationships. No more going nowhere with my writing—I invested in myself, tolerating only high-frequency behaviors that led me to gain tens of thousands of followers in a few short months. No more

bad sleep every night—I cut back heavily on caffeine (I had been drinking an average of six to eight cups of coffee a day) and staying up late watching TV. My sleep is better today than it has been the past four years.

If you tolerate mediocrity, that's exactly what you'll get. I've learned life is constantly testing you, seeing what you'll put up with. Typically, you get what you accept, and if you take the first lowball offer you're presented with, that's as high as you'll go. Want a better relationship, income, health, sleep quality, car, house, clothes, influence? Then refuse the mediocre offer and negotiate for the top-tier one.

PART 3.

Life Free of the Trap: Creating a Winning Mindset

CONGRATULATIONS. IF YOU'RE READING this, it means you're one of the few of us who made it out of the cage. The good news? You never have to go back. You know too much. Once you're aware of the trap, you can always avoid it—for good.

Still, we'll always have the choice to go back to our mediocre routines. Many people have an intimate understanding of how mediocre their lives are yet don't do anything about them. It can be easy to

unknowingly slip back into the prison you've worked
so hard to escape.

The following chapters are your strategy guide for
freedom: how to be consistent, what skills you need to
develop, how to focus on personal growth when all you
want to do is sleep in, watch TV, and shove your face
into the nearest source of chocolate.

CONSISTENCY

"Most people knock on the door of their dreams once, then run away before anyone has a chance to open the door. But if you keep knocking, persistently and endlessly, eventually the door will open."

—LES BROWN

CONSISTENCY IS WHAT SEPARATES the wannabes from the genuine article, the people who will *actually* succeed. Without consistency, you will not sustain any meaningful change or new lifestyle. To escape mediocrity, you must learn how to be consistent, a rare trait indeed.

Why It's So Hard to Be Consistent

"Ninety-five percent of our society—the 'mediocre majority'—fail, time and time again, to start exercise routines, quit smoking, improve their diets, stick to a budget, or any other life habit that would improve their quality of life. Why? Most people don't realize the seemingly unbearable first ten days of a new habit is only temporary."

—HAL ELROD

Everything is hard before it's easy. Those who are successful in their progress are the ones who pushed through the initial difficult few weeks of a new change until it became bearable, even commonplace. Consistency is most difficult at the beginning; if you can get through the first rough patches, you're already ahead of 90 percent of the competition.

I've been writing for many years. The first four and a half years of intense blogging, I had basically nothing to show for it—fewer than two hundred subscribers, a few dozen views a day, and $40 in earned income (total).

Around year five, everything changed. I began attracting three to four thousand subscribers…a month. I went from one hundred views a day to two hundred thousand views a month. I began making online courses and selling them for thousands of dollars. What happened? I became consistent.

Looking back on those first four and a half years of passionate, zealous blogging, I had to admit I was never consistent. Like most amateur writers, I would write several articles for a few weeks. Upon seeing that no one was reading them, I'd fall into a self-loathing depression and stop writing for months. Then I'd repeat the cycle.

Then, I finally decided to be consistent. I reached

the point where I was so disgusted with my lack of progress, I committed to writing every single day. After the first month, I had more views than any other month. The next few months of consistent, daily writing brought a meteoric rise of influence for me, eventually leading me to be one of the top writers on Medium, a popular blogging hub.

Until you're consistent, you'll never get what you want.

Imagine an alcoholic who knows she needs to stop drinking. She vows to not drink the entire day. But she tells herself she can drink for five minutes at the end of the day, as a reward.

The entire day, that little treat—the cheat meal, the sugary coffee, a little porn, a little bit of drugs— hangs over your head. That's all you can think about. In a twisted way, the source of the problem actually becomes the source of motivation.

Giving yourself this little out makes the process of quitting one hundred times harder.

97 Percent Is Harder Than 100 Percent

> "If you want lasting change, you have to give up this idea of just trying something, and you have to commit yourself to mastery. That means not just "dabbling," but fully immersing yourself. Because your life is not controlled by what you do some of the time, but by what you do consistently."
>
> —TONY ROBBINS

If you want to truly change any behavior, you need to let go of this idea of 97 percent and commit to 100 percent.

You need to stop dabbling and actually commit. You need to be consistent. Otherwise, you'll always be wasting energy trying to motivate yourself.

Most people dabble. They promise they'll be good, but they leave themselves an out. This little safety net is a powerful message to their mind that says, "I probably can't do this task."

This message becomes incredibly powerful in your subconscious. Author David Schwartz described it like this: "Disbelief is negative power. When the mind disbelieves or doubts, the mind attracts 'reasons' to support the disbelief."

Alcoholics Anonymous describes how many new alcoholics often hide bottles, saving secret booze as they pretend to look sober. To the outside observer, there's no more alcohol. But it's a lie.

You are more powerful than you think. You don't need hidden bottles and safety nets.

You'll be OK. The process of evolving into a better version of yourself feels like you're literally killing off parts of you.

The truth is, you are. But that's OK. You're killing off the old so the new can thrive.

How to Be Consistent

"Repetition can be boring or tedious—which is why so few people ever master anything."

—HAL ELROD

I can't make you consistent. No one can. There are thousands of self-improvement books out there, and none of them can make you consistent, this one included. Either you're serious, or you're not.

What I can do is teach you the principles for sustaining that choice.

The world's best performers are consistent. It's one of their fundamental virtues. In his autobiography, Hall of Fame NBA player Ray Allen explained his pregame routine was unalterable and sacred. If someone even parked in his parking space before the gym, his whole routine could be derailed. The most decorated Olympic athlete of all time, Michael Phelps, once said the only time he ever deviated from his schedule was one time,

where his coach let him leave fifteen minutes early to attend his school dance. Paulo Coelho, author of *The Alchemist* (65 million copies sold), still publishes a book every two years.

Having a hard time being consistent? Welcome to the club. It's tough. Most people can't do it.

The ability to be consistent lies in your choice beforehand. If you don't predetermine when you'll quit, you'll always end up quitting sooner than you needed to.

A young stand-up comic once revealed a conversation with comedian Jerry Seinfeld about how Seinfeld was so consistent:

He told me to get a big wall calendar that has a whole year on one page and hang it on a prominent wall. The next step was to get a big red magic marker.

He said for each day that I do my task of writing, I get to put a big red X over that day. "After a few days you'll have a chain. Just keep at it and the chain will grow longer every day. You'll like seeing that chain, especially when you get a few weeks under your belt. Your only job next is to not break the chain."

Don't break the chain. Just make your X, every day.

FOCUS ON LEARNING AND CREATING

"Every skill you acquire doubles your odds of success."

—SCOTT ADAMS

THE MORE YOU LEARN, the more you expand your abilities. Not only that, you learn *how* to learn—how to read books faster, cook better, jog longer. The more these abilities expand, the more you can recognize opportunities that will make your life more extraordinary. If you focus on learning and creating, you'll learn how to recognize and seize these opportunities.

There is no limit to how much you can learn, and contrary to popular opinion, there is no limit to what skills you can acquire. Fly-fishing, podcasting, life coaching, networking, dribbling a basketball, radio repair, knitting, Google Adwords, communicating with your partner—all these are useful in making your highest dreams a reality, because all skills are connected.

Justine Musk, author and TEDx speaker (and first wife of Elon Musk), once described this idea:

When you become a master of two worlds (say, engineering and business), you can bring them together in a way that will a) introduce hot ideas to each other, so they can have idea sex and make idea babies that no one has seen before and b) create a competitive advantage because you can move between

worlds, speak both languages, connect the tribes, mash the elements to spark fresh creative insight until you wake up with the epiphany that changes your life.

This revelation is huge. Just like two ideas, two skills can equal more than the sum of their individual parts. Your ability to expertly maneuver through traffic and your skill at board games are connected. So are your marketing expertise and tennis ability. So are your abilities to stir-fry khao soi and empathize with your partner.

A single Clydesdale horse can pull a load up to eight thousand pounds. Two horses pulling together don't pull twice as much; they can actually pull three times as much. The two horses that can each pull eight thousand pounds alone can pull twenty-four thousand pounds working together.

Skills (and ideas) are powerful, but combining them creates disproportionately more momentum than the simple sum of each one. Skills become sharper and more expansive when combined with other skills. One area of your life invariably affects every other area—how you do anything is how you do everything. If you focus on learning and creating new skills and abilities, you can begin combining these into developments that will truly separate you from the rest of the world.

The masses do the opposite—indulge in entertainment and distraction, letting their brains decay on autopilot. TV, alcohol, sex, sleep, and other common mind escapes aren't inherently bad; the problem is that most people aren't responsible enough to use these to effectively relax. They overdo it, deadening their vitality and becoming more tired, more bored, and more restless.

Prolific author C. S. Lewis once described humans this way: "We are like eggs at present. And you cannot go on indefinitely being just an ordinary, decent egg. We must be hatched or go bad." In a way, you are always in the state of an egg; you are either hatching and growing or stagnating and going bad. What you focus on is magnified; seek learning and creating, and opportunities will come to make that happen. As author Paulo Coelho once wrote, "When you want something, all the universe conspires in helping you to achieve it." We gain what we focus on.

The ordinary person seeks out entertainment and distraction. They get what they seek—entertainment and distraction in all forms produces trillions of dollars every year. But what do they get in return? If you seek entertainment and distraction as your primary goals— "working for the weekend," so to speak—you may get them. But is that the life you want? Trudging your way through your days, doing the bare minimum so you won't get fired, holding your breath until Friday at 4:30 p.m.? This reflects in your relationships, income, career, family, and mindset.

The extraordinary individual focuses on learning and creating. Successful individuals understand this is how they propel themselves into relationships with other top-tier individuals, develop world-class routines, and move ever closer to living their ideal life.

Whatever your goal is—to become 100 percent financially independent, to fit into your wedding dress again, to run a six-minute mile—these goals invariably require many skills you've never mastered. If you want what you've never had, you must do what you've never done.

When I first started writing, I had a goal to make writing my full-time career. I was sick of the nine-to-five grind; I wanted my own business. But how to make money? Turns out there are dozens of ways I could earn money...which meant dozens of new skills I had to learn. Of the various skills I've learned, I managed to figure out:

- ▶ How to create and set up a podcast
- ▶ How to create an online course
- ▶ How to sell products to my email list
- ▶ How to set up website hosting

▶ How to meet other writers and become friends with them

▶ How to write a book

▶ How to change my name servers for my website so I could add virus protection

▶ How to code an email capture box

When I started, I couldn't do any of these. Now, I've gained innumerable skills—coding, software development, sales savvy, relationship building, website creation, the ability to talk with tech support… all skills that have led me to other opportunities. I meet another writer, and we talk about how annoying it is to set up a podcast, creating rapport and friendship. I create a cool new course and know how to actually sell it, prompting readers to pay me for coaching services.

In the words of Jim Rohn, "Formal education will make you a living; self-education will make you a fortune."

11.

TREAT YOURSELF LIKE THE HERO
(AND WORK YOUR ASS OFF)

"The key to becoming world-class in your
endeavors is to build your performance around
world-class routines."

—DARREN HARDY

WHEN ARNOLD SCHWARZENEGGER CAME to America with no
money, a heavy foreign accent, and dreams of becoming a leading man in Hollywood, the only roles he was
offered were amateur, lesser roles—crude villains like

Nazi officers and evil henchmen with no lines. All everyone saw was a foreigner with big muscles.

His agent begged him to take the roles. What else could a poor immigrant actor with the unreadable last name Schwarzenegger hope for?

But he refused. He wanted to be the hero, the leading man, and wouldn't settle for anything less. So he treated himself like one. He invested in himself, taking acting, speech, and voice classes from renowned coaches and trainers. He worked as a bricklayer on the side to support his acting dreams. He met as many high-profile actors as he could and asked them countless questions on how to do what they do. Years after becoming the most famous leading actor in Hollywood (and the world), Schwarzenegger wrote, "The only way you become a leading man is to treat yourself like a leading man and work your ass off."

You'll always slip back into lesser versions of yourself if you don't treat yourself like a better version.

Tony Robbins once used the following analogy to

describe this principle. Say you're in a room with an air-conditioner. The AC will always attempt to bring the room temperature to whatever temperature you set it to. For instance, if you set the AC to seventy degrees, the AC will attempt to heat/cool the room accordingly.

In the same way, you set the temperature of your own mind. If you set it low (say, sixty-eight degrees), your mind will always be attempting to bring you down to that internal number. Even if you have an opportunity to grow—a possible promotion opens up, a business investment falls in your lap, a potential incredible dating partner enters your life—your mind will literally prevent you from reaching a higher temperature or reality. Your mind follows what you tell it. In the words of bestselling author Joseph Murphy, "Your subconscious mind takes the orders you give it based on what your conscious mind believes and accepts as true." This analogy describes how we so often limit ourselves, even sabotage our own efforts to succeed, because our self-belief is not high enough.

You may think the phrase "afraid of succeeding" is silly. I did. But then I started thinking about what it would really be like if I succeeded as a writer. What if people bought my book...and hated it? What if word spread that I was a terrible author? "You only get one shot, you know," said the voice in the back of my head. Or what if people bought my online courses, hated them, and then sued me? These fears had been there since the beginning and reflected my low internal temperature number. The ways I diabolically sabotaged my own success became obvious—procrastinating, delaying, even "forgetting" to send important emails and manage time-sensitive problems.

If your internal temperature number is low, it doesn't matter how much work you do or what opportunities come your way. You will only reach the temperature that you set—high or low as that may be—and your mind will do all it can to get there, even self-sabotage. This is why it's so important to treat yourself like the hero. Set your internal temperature really high, and your mind will follow with your actions, choices, and behaviors.

This is how a penniless immigrant with a thick accent can rise through the ranks of the most competitive industry in the world and succeed as number one. Schwarzenegger's internal temperature was extremely high, and his actions reflected that.

▶ What beliefs are limiting you?

▶ Why don't you think you can do it?

▶ Do you believe you can become rich and wealthy?

▶ Or have a happy, fun marriage that will never end in divorce?

▶ Open your own business and become your own boss?

▶ Write your book?

▶ Start your podcast?

▶ Be an incredible parent with kids who love and respect you?

▶ Cut out sugar from your diet?

You can do any of these things. Set your temperature high, and your mind will follow.

When You Believe, You Act Differently

"He believes he is among the best, and so he acts and performs the best."

—DAVID SCHWARTZ

In his autobiography, Hall of Fame NBA player Ray Allen reflected on a team he had been on. They were talented, but it was obvious they didn't believe they could win. Some players intentionally hunted for stats, padding their individual accomplishments to save face if the team lost. The locker room was a bleak, hostile environment. Deep down, the team didn't believe they could win the championship, and they acted like it.

For the first four and a half years of my writing, I made no progress. No followers, no views, no income.

Looking back, it's obvious I saw myself as a mediocre writer. I didn't believe I was talented or professional or an expert. I treated myself as a mediocre blogger, so that's how I acted. I didn't invest in myself, and I never bought books, took courses, or studied my craft. Subconsciously, I was probably thinking, "Why spend the money? It's a lost cause anyway."

I finally got disgusted enough with mediocrity that I decided to change. I bought a small $19 online course on journaling. Then I bought books. I began studying top authors and dissecting their articles. I made grids and notes on several top writers with boxes that track their word count, quotes per post, links, length of paragraphs, etc. I bought a $500 writing course. The ball was rollin'.

Now, I treat myself like a top writer. Because what do top writers do? They invest in themselves. They don't tolerate mediocrity. They can brutally edit their self-indulgent ramblings. They expect to win. In the words of one of the greatest athletes of all time, Michael Jordan, "You have to expect things of yourself before you can do them." Bruce Lee, arguably the most famous martial artist in history, put it this way: "One will never get any more than he thinks he can get."

Treat yourself like the hero.

(And work your ass off.)

BEHAVE LIKE SUCCESSFUL PEOPLE BEHAVE

"If you want to live an exceptional and extraordinary life, you have to give up many of the things that are part of a normal one."

—SRINIVAS RAO

THE MOST SUCCESSFUL PEOPLE in the world act extraordinarily differently from the average person.

Author Tim Ferriss interviewed literally hundreds of the world's most successful athletes, entrepreneurs, performers, actors, politicians, writers, and thought leaders in his book *Tools of Titans: The Tactics, Routines, and Habits of Billionaires, Icons, and World-Class Performers.* He compiled a list of some common findings. For instance:

▶ More than 80 percent of the interviewees have some form of daily mindfulness or meditation practice.

▶ Almost all interviewees have done spec work (completing projects on their own time and dollar, then submitting them to prospective buyers).

▶ The interviewees have the shared belief that "failure is not durable" (consistent action will eventually enable success).

▶ Almost every interviewee has taken time to specifically work on turning weaknesses into advantages.

If you flip through the hundreds of interviews in the book (and hundreds more in Ferriss's follow-up book of interviews, *Tribe of Mentors: Short Life Advice from the Best in the World*), you begin to get an idea of what successful people do, and you realize their actions, habits, behaviors, choices, beliefs, and principles are often radically different from the norm in nearly every area—health, career, relationships, finances, success, ability, and mindset.

If you want to become extraordinary, do what successful people do.

You Have No Excuse Not to Read Books

> "The fellow who has gone nowhere and has no plans for getting anywhere always has a bookful of reasons to explain why."
>
> —DAVID SCHWARTZ

Tony Robbins has revealed he's read over seven hundred books in his field. Warren Buffett claims to read five to six hours a day. Mark Zuckerberg, Bill

Gates, Mark Cuban, and Elon Musk have famously stated they read around a book a week, consistently. A popular study by *Fast Company* reports CEOs read an average of sixty books a year. The enormous amount of additional research on reading books makes the message clear: those who achieve a lot read a lot.

As a writer in particular, you need to read a lot of books to improve your writing. The other day, I was speaking with a friend of mine, an amateur writer. I asked him what books he's been reading. "I don't read books," he stated flatly. "I'm too slow, and I can never finish them." This is what unsuccessful people chant to themselves. Remember, what you believe is what you become.

Writer or not, if you want to be successful, then do what successful people do—read books. Maybe you've never called yourself a reader. Many people stop reading entirely after college. That's OK. You can start whenever you want. It just means you'll probably have a slow go at first, as with any new habit. In addition to the straightforward "successful people read books" idea, there are countless other benefits:

- ▶ Reduced stress
- ▶ Increased memory capacity
- ▶ Increased vocabulary
- ▶ Stronger analytical skills
- ▶ More potential talking points in conversation
- ▶ Improved focus
- ▶ Upgraded writing skills
- ▶ Better sleep quality (studies especially recommend reading fiction before bed)

Ordinary People Consume; Elite People Study Their Craft

"Mental resilience is arguably the most critical trait of a world-class performer, and it should be nurtured continuously. Left to my own devices, I am always looking for more ways to become more and more psychologically impregnable. When uncomfortable, my instinct is not to avoid the discomfort but to become at peace with it... My instinct is always to seek out challenges as opposed to avoiding them."

—JOSH WAITZKIN

Most people aren't concerned with learning, growing, and evolving into better versions of themselves. Successful people are constantly evolving, and they do that by studying their craft.

NBA All-Star DeAndre Jordan once recounted a story from his rookie year in the NBA. He was tasked

with guarding Hall of Fame power forward Tim Duncan. Jordan was nervous and easily rattled, and he was easily outplayed by Duncan.

One of his veteran teammates, Marcus Camby, pulled him aside after the game and asked a question.

"What's Tim's favorite move?"

"I dunno," I told him.

Marcus was straight-up shocked by my response.

"You mean you just went out there and guessed?" he said, looking at me like I was an alien or something.

That was a real eye-opening moment for me. As a rookie, I never thought too much about who we were playing the next night. I knew who I had to guard, but Marcus encouraged me—in kind of an intimidating way—to go deeper. He made it into a game between us. He'd ask me to study the tendencies of players and then pepper me with follow-up questions. *Which hand does he shoot with when he's on the left low block? The right block? Which way does he like to spin? Does he pump-fake? Does he do an up-and-under?*

In what scenarios? How can you tell he's going to do it? It was all really specific stuff.

This is how the world's most successful people approach their craft. They don't strut in, try their best, and leave. They become students of their game.

Your Level of Success Is Determined by Your Level of Investment

"The extent of the struggle determines the extent of the growth."

—RYAN HOLIDAY

Research has shown as many as 50 percent of people haven't read more than a handful of books after college. Fewer than half of people with gym memberships go consistently!

These and many other telling studies point to a simple fact.

Most people stop improving.

But world-class winners never stop.

When it comes to improving, world-class winners are fanatical about always getting better. They understand their ability to grow and evolve directly determines their ability to operate at peak levels.

World-class winners know they are never done. You never arrive at a new behavior; you simply become better and better.

The more you improve, the more opportunities will become available. As numerous people have said, "The more I practice, the luckier I get."

WHY YOU SHOULDN'T TAKE ADVICE FROM (ALMOST) ANYONE

"Advice is one thing that is freely given away, but watch that you take only what is worth having. He who takes advice about his savings from one who is inexperienced in such matters shall pay with his savings for proving the falsity of their opinions."

—GEORGE CLASON

MOST OF THE PEOPLE you know have no idea how to achieve the goals you have.

This doesn't stop people from giving advice though. In fact, a lack of knowledge seems to spur people to give advice even more. The truth is, most people would rather choose to feel important than admit they don't know the answer.

I saw this a lot when I graduated from college. Everyone wanted to tell me what to do with my career and how to do it. But looking back, pretty much all these advice givers were stuck in the same place as everyone else: broke, in debt, and bored at a lousy job.

Former editor-in-chief of *SUCCESS* magazine, Darren Hardy, once said, "Never ask advice of someone with whom you wouldn't want to trade places."

You shouldn't take advice from almost anyone, because so few people know how to get where you want to go.

Never Take Advice from Sources That Can Only Offer Mediocre Information

"The mediocre have a very narrow perception of reality, and in turn, their lives. They see things as they are, not how they *can* be."

—ADITYA MEHTA

I have a pretty lofty set of goals. Some of them are things like:

▶ Become 100 percent financially independent
▶ Earn $200,000 this year from my writing
▶ Have an incredibly fulfilling and intimate marriage
▶ Write my first traditionally published book this year

Most of the people in my life haven't achieved these goals. That's OK; it just means I shouldn't go to them looking for answers. I can't trust sources that can only give me subpar advice.

My parents' marriage ended in cheating and divorce. I love them, but I need a different source of information for marital success. None of my colleagues at my old corporate job were making anything close to the income I want. Why would I go to them for financial advice?

In his classic parable *The Richest Man in Babylon*, George S. Clason wrote:

Why trust the knowledge of a brick maker about jewels? Would you go to the bread maker to inquire about the stars?

No, by my tunic, you would go to the astronomer, if you had power to think... And next time if you would have advice about jewels, go to the jewel merchant. If you would know the truth about sheep, go to the herdsman.

If you follow the advice of clueless people, you'll end up just like them.

This is why I take advice from very few people. It's not that I'm too smart or that I know everything already. On the contrary, I need all the wisdom I can get. I just choose my sources carefully. I typically only follow the guidance of those who have (or know how to get) what I want.

When I first joined a twelve-step program for pornography addiction, my therapist told me to get a sponsor, someone to help guide me.

"Well, who should I ask?" I asked, bewildered.

His answer was simple: find someone who has what you want. Then follow everything they say. I ended up connecting with an old-timer with over thirty years of sobriety. His wisdom is proven, and his methods are sound. He had what I wanted, so I followed him. If you want an extraordinary life, be extremely selective with whom you go to for counsel and guidance.

The More Selective You Are, the Better Training You'll Get

The loudest voices rarely offer the best wisdom.

It can be tempting to go with these teachings; many do. But one of the lessons I learned after reading all the top finance books available was that if you follow traditional advice, you'll get average (see: mediocre) results.

The same is true for any endeavor. In reality, it's often the quiet, softer-spoken individuals who have the knowledge you need. In the words of author Mokokoma Mokhonoana, "The more you know, the less you talk. The less you talk, the more you know."

▶ Have you been following average, commonsense advice?

▶ Where are you headed?

▶ Are you confident you'll end up in a place you want to be?

▶ Whom do you go to for advice?

The more selective you are, the better training and advice you'll receive. Don't absorb advice and instructions from countless individuals who can only offer mediocre, average information. If you want better advice, be selective instead.

The truth is, most people in your life have no idea how to get where you want to go.

Be selective with where you get your information. Trust yourself. When in doubt, take a step forward. Small progress, every day.

If you want what no one else has, you must do what no one else does. Seek out the right teachers and training. For every source, ask yourself: Do they have what I want?

14.

WELCOME TO LIFE OUTSIDE OF MEDIOCRE

"How much you improve is up to you."

—ANDERS ERICSSON

LIFE ISN'T BLACK AND white. It's not that simple.

There will be times when you will find yourself not doing what you need to do to succeed, to stay out of mediocrity. You'll sleep through your alarm, eat that bad food, skip important work sessions, and let your gym membership collect dust.

The goal is progress, not perfection. You will never arrive at your final plateau. You have the choice to improve and evolve until your dying day. As Anders Ericsson, Swedish psychologist and pioneer of the principle of Deliberate Practice, once wrote, "There is no point at which performance maxes out and additional practice does not lead to further improvement."

It's easy to slip back into mediocre behaviors. No one is perfect. The best we can do is continually try to progress toward our goal. That's enough—to do the best we can with what we have.

You may not think you're doing it right. You may find yourself thinking you're not doing enough, that the little actions you're taking mean nothing.

Tim Ferriss once wrote, "10x results don't always require 10x effort. Big changes can come in small packages." In his book *The Compound Effect*, Darren Hardy wrote, "Small, seemingly insignificant steps completed consistently over time will create a radical difference."

The most important part of staying out of mediocrity and continuing to excel is to be consistent—even when it feels like you're getting nowhere. This is how extraordinary athletes, entrepreneurs, performers, and leaders rose so high in their fields; they kept going when everyone else quit. They kept going when there was seemingly no evidence of improvement. They kept going when everyone had given up on them.

The Reward for Your Efforts

Mediocrity is exhausting. It's extraordinarily tiring to continue wallowing in a subpar job, relationship, and place in life.

But here's what happens when you decide to upgrade from ordinary to extraordinary.

Life gets bigger. Like, *way* bigger.

In her book *Mindset: The New Psychology of Success*, Dr. Carol Dweck describes the "growth mindset" as the belief "that effort or training can change one's qualities and traits." It means you become whatever you want. You can be as good, as skilled, and capable as you make yourself to be.

You Can Be Anything

Growing up, my parents went bankrupt, and we lost everything—the trucks, the car, the motorcycle, the house, the family business. All gone. I had to ask my high school friend if I could move in with him for the last two weeks before graduation because the rest of my family couldn't fit into my grandpa's tiny house.

This enforced a simple truth I accepted as fact: that I would never have financial stability. The most I could hope for would be an average salary with benefits and a decent house. I would never be free of worry; I would always have the specter of bankruptcy and family ruin on my heels. Oh well.

After I did the work to upgrade my mindset and I realized I could be whatever I want, the entire world

opened up. I could be my own boss and make hundreds of thousands of dollars a year in passive income. I could have an incredibly successful marriage with no hiding, no secrets, and no fear of divorce. I could be a better speaker and work on my stuttering so that it could be virtually nonexistent. I could be *anything*.

It might sound silly. It feels silly to write it. But the feeling is intoxicating. How much you improve is up to you. You can go as far and get as big as you want—if you're willing to do the work.

Life outside of mediocre is not crowded, yet the opportunities expanded a thousand times. Tim Ferriss put it this way: "It's lonely at the top. 99 percent of people are convinced they are incapable of achieving great things, so they aim for the mediocre middle ground. The level of competition is thus fiercest for 'realistic' goals, paradoxically making them the most time- and energy-consuming."

Before, I was trying to be the best of the average Joes. I was gunning for that 3 percent pay increase, busting my ass for the title of "lead fill-in-the-blank," and ascending the ladder of mediocrity as fast as I could.

Now, I realize I can skip steps, even skip the entire game. I don't compete with anyone; everyone competes with me. A couple of years ago, I was still in the midst of my mediocre writing; it was *so hard* to wake up at 7:00 a.m. to write. Now, it's weird—I *like* 5:00 a.m. I'm excited for the day, because I'm building the life I actually want to live, not someone else's version. I've cut out negative people from my life. I don't gossip, complain, or criticize anymore (for the most part). I don't look at those more successful than me with disdain and toxic jealousy; I applaud them and am inspired by them.

I know I'll get there one day.

ACKNOWLEDGMENTS

I CAN'T DESCRIBE HOW thankful I am for my team at Sourcebooks. Thank you so much to Meg Gibbons, Grace Menary-Winefield, and the entire editing/design team that helped bring this book to light. To Kimi—thanks for helping me write this book by always encouraging me and reminding me that yes, I would finish it someday. And mom—thanks for correcting all my typos.

ABOUT THE AUTHOR

ANTHONY MOORE is a top writer on Medium for personal growth and self-improvement. He has an MA in psychology and lives in California.

NEW! Only from Simple Truths®

IGNITE READS
spark impact in just one hour

IGNITE READS IS A NEW SERIES OF 1-HOUR READS WRITTEN BY WORLD-RENOWNED EXPERTS!

These captivating books will help you become the best version of yourself, allowing for new opportunities in your personal and professional life. Accelerate your career and expand your knowledge with these powerful books written on today's hottest ideas.

TRENDING BUSINESS AND PERSONAL GROWTH TOPICS

 Read in an hour or less

 Leading experts and authors

 Bold design and captivating content